WALKING TOWARD CRANES

Amy Small-McKinney

Amy Small-McKinney

GLASS LYRE PRESS

Paperback ISBN: 978-1-941783-29-0

Cover art: © Lioraa | Dreamstime.com
Author Photo: Jennifer Kertis-Veit
Design & layout: Steven Asmussen
Copyediting: Linda E. Kim

Glass Lyre Press, LLC
P.O. Box 2693
Glenview, IL 60025
www.GlassLyrePress.com

ACKNOWLEDGMENTS

The American Poetry Review: Background; Building Collapse

arc—24: Entry

APIARY # 8, Soft Targets Issue: Inside The World

BARED: Contemporary Poetry and Art on Bras and Breasts, edited by Laura Madeline Wiseman (Les Femme Folles Books): An Apple, Cut; Central Park

Cortland Review: American Dream/Legacy

Les Femme Folles Press: The Matter of Beginning

Philadelphia Stories (Honorable Mention): Self as a Bog

Tiferet, Literature, Art, & The Creative Spirit: Stone; Where We Live

Grateful acknowledgement to poets Leonard Gontarek and Liz Chang for their close readings of my manuscript.

WALKING TOWARD CRANES

winner of the 2016 Kithara Book Prize

The *kithara* was an ancient Greek musical instrument in the lyre family used for solo playing, as well as to accompany poetry and song.

Previous Winners

CONTENTS

THE HEALING

WALKING TOWARD CRANES

for Russ & Sarah

1
TREATMENT

BACKGROUND

My soul moves toward its fifth season.
Smoke rises from fires burned years ago.
A soul is not a door or summer or fireplace or dog.
There is a door. Behind it a painted chair, navy, red,
a rug hand-woven yellow. A dog with its head on a lap,
the lap forgiving. One foot shifts back and forth
trying to rid itself of a slipper.
In the background, a fireplace without a fire,
because summer is coming and azaleas are purple
and books are everywhere. Summer is a book.
A woman, the central character, withdraws from the world,
on her land, a school is rebuilt.
Who am I becoming? I am not a school.

Flying Low

What are those birds called
that flew in front of my car,

black dots, floaters in an eye?
Near my home, I was driving home,

when a swarm flew so low
I almost hit them,
had to look behind and swerve.

One tried to talk to me.
If I listened, I would know he is tired.

Inside of me, there is a swarm,
surplus only heat will destroy.

My body close to a dishonest sun.
The solution is simple.

Point out wingspan, flight pattern, color.
Measure, calibrate, name.

If he listens, I will tell him,
I don't want to give up.

I pretend he is a young thing, will fly forever,
blackbird.

AN APPLE, CUT

Empty space is fine, I mean valuable.

A stranger has entered my home, refuses to leave.

He dared to unlock the door, let himself in.

You know by now this is metaphor.

I don't know what else to say

about waiting to be carved into, emptied out, stitched.

These breasts fed my child for almost two years.

~

I am more than food.

The artist painted a likeness of my body.

I was not ashamed.

I was his bowl of uncut apples.

~

Mitosis, epidermal receptor, staging,

grading, a new vocabulary. Two weeks ago, pointless.

    Now, I burn. I call this fire.
    They call it headway.

When my daughter was born, I opened into a basin, received her, cool water.

    ~

The first line is about crossing a river.

I want to know exactly which river

I am to cross. Look, I don't want to die,

probably won't. Here is the river.

I found it inside a book of poems, inside my own house.

~

I have always been afraid of water.

From the beginning, I only learned to swim

because a woman with brown hair held my hands

and would not let go.

My body was skinny, all knees, no breasts.

Suanna was afraid.

She was the most beautiful girl I had ever seen.

How could a beautiful girl be afraid?

Fourteen Days After Treatment

I wanted it shaved
when the first bunch fell into my hands,
onto the shower floor. A kind of badge.
But my head is tinier than I imagined
and my ears pop out.
Last night, I joked, "Paging Spock."
I said it because I stood there, in front of him.
This morning, before he woke up,
I uncovered my head
to know how it feels
to sit in a chair, to read a paper,
then bound myself with a blue cotton headscarf.
When I was a girl, I used my hair as a kind of weapon.
It hung to my waist in cheeky waves.
I swear I didn't know it would be gone,
that people we love leave, our own bodies leave.
I think about movies and baldheaded women
who slept with German soldiers or women
in camps and bottomless snow.
It is chilly in my house. I bought
a teal cotton cap for sleeping, I won't be cold.

INSIDE THE WORLD

I am afraid to leave my house.
Since it arrived with its steel gray suitcase,
its passport with permits from everywhere.
Now, it goes with me everywhere.
I feel safer when we are indoors, windows
locked, doors locked, a husband working
nearby on a puzzle called Planet Earth
with one thousand tiny pieces that will become
the Boreal Forest in Lapland though when I looked
it up I read that this *taiga* spreads into
Finland and Sweden and Russia though
I may be wrong or misunderstand borders.
That's cancer.
Every day my body is a different place.
My real life hides in trees, beneath deep snow.
If I open my door, the wind will divide me.

Post-Minimalist

Inside a hollowed out body, what is left?

Yellow, in all likelihood. Yellow is not hope, not defector.
It is a woman and her art, water and gas.

If my body disappears, someone will hear me inside walls
scrambling toward green. Or in a door as it opens.

If this is not about death, and it is not, it is about color.
What it remembers.

I am probably red, though not blood,
because I retreat, wave a white flag,

separate myself from a violet body.

Red sky breaks from night.

Here is what I know.

BODY

Of course, bed, sink, shoes.
She wants to wake up,
to be four walls, a window,
emptied of everything except hope.
That she will keep.

That was it. In the middle of the night,
room already dark, but no, this was darkness,
half her life momentarily vanished,
a tiny clot roamed away from its tumor.
A wing tucked under. A kiss.
A redbird sailed into glass, discovered an eye.

Years ago, she dropped beneath a desk awaiting bombs.
She had blond hair.
The teacher said they might come someday.
This is someday, her body nuclear.

With wire strung inside a breast, smelling salts,
a lymph node carried off to pathology.
A yellow rubber duck rests on the edge of a tub.

Meanwhile, it is not enough to add unasked-for cells
to her right breast! Not enough
to blind the right eye, twice.
She waits to forget you, dangerous body.

But, there is no she,
talking to air, elements, even water not enough.
Though she forced her husband away, walked by soft fronds
she once feathered across their daughter's young mouth.
Then a mailbox, just a mailbox, with news that is more than *just*.
The quiet almost buried her.

There is no she, only her that once lived in a furious city,
built bars around windows.
Less keeping out, more keeping in, the safety
of floral curtains with tiebacks, memory of water
from a green hose.

Last night, I finally cried, my dead father
touched my cheek, my cheek.
I said, Afraid.

Learning to Float

Cells swim, probably singing, toward a sweet shore.

Taxotere rips them from lung and liver.

Bone marrow swells into white rooms.

On the white couch, arms, toes, eyelids, every part gives in.

I let him sleep.

He does not need to count these contractions.

I need a mother.

LEGER, AFTER TREATMENT

My body is not his Paris.
There are no lights.

I contain a *law of contrasts*—
I was flawless suburbia, sprawl, then blight.

I am an entire country with a barrier wall that splits.
Love walks into my river, stones secured to its limbs.

Lost, every color, element, self.

HERE TO THERE
for K

1.

She says, God has always been here.
Well, God does not decide who will live or die.

2.

When the body is rampaging, by the way,
why care about scars or hair or who we are in the universe?
Those black coats. I wore them, my heart was wool.
Beneath, something lighter.
Not skin. Believe me, not a soul.

3.

Today, the market.
Fresh fruit, green vegetables,
hope, a green apple.
He strokes my head, tenderly.
Your hair is coming back.

4.

Yes, yes, I am clean of disease!

What is left: seven months it took to get here.
If treatment doesn't kill you, it will cure you.

I was a twig, defenseless.

5.

The men removed my fallen trees.
Snow again on Tuesday.
Seven more days
of radiation.
My breast is leather, tanned,
burns.
In the meantime, I am not noble.

6.

I have a friend.
The treatment has not killed what grows.
I cannot be her, I sit beside her.
She wears a silk blouse,
embroidered with fish and loaves.

7.

I am beginning to remember my body.
I will wake up tomorrow. I am not a leaf.
This is good. As good as throat singing,
uneven noise of being alive.

WINTER

The world is becoming sadder.

One eye opened is enough
to see a couch, a cat, someone asleep,
or choose nothing.

Where were you when you first read *A Child's Christmas in Wales?*

You understand the necessity of detail,
words as wind, winter as deception.

Every December, it parks itself onto your chest, swears it loves you.
If it did, it would not force you to drink from its spring
as though holy and you still thirsty.

Every year, the same story, how as a child
you would have given your voice to be loved.

You hear static and then a voice.
It is someone from long ago, she tells you she loves you too.
She is going to rest now, her head on a rose colored pillow,
a man beside her, biding his time.

Okay, you tell her, and you are lying.

You want to push back, freeze everything, back, yourself, back.
This is not a dream. Do not consider the possibility.

How else to explain your body a platform for travelers or despair?
Or the Dead Sea where nothing can swim, nothing can drown?

How it murmurs to you or sings siren songs
or crushes you and that is closer to the truth.

You drink its water, inky. You stand up.
Look out the window, trees rightly bare.

For R

sentimental but lovely

When I am dead, you will still be my lamb, I will hear you bleating.
In your bed, when you are jolted awake by the usual neighbors, police cars,
I will finally move toward you, undefended, I will be headlights in the dark.
By your bed, I will be the green light, always on, faxing from your faulty heart.
In the morning, I will be the car that drives you to the creek, the bench,
where you watch walkers, not lambs, move across a steel bridge, sturdy.
If you are holding a book, and you will be, it will be *The Sparrow.*
I will be the alien I refused to read about in life. I couldn't give you that.
Instead, I wanted to move back, into black and white, the pewter pitcher,
a pigeon on the bowler hat.
I promise you, I will be the other, the one you long to talk to.

after Muriel Rukeyser

18

NATASHA

I live in a farmhouse, by a road, with a woman who languishes in bed.
It was a Thursday when I ran toward thickets, remnants of the great outdoors.
The black Volvo sped away.

Blood poured over me, as though I were a cup and god was drinking.
I could not get up, a crushed tick on tarmac, until a thread pulled at me,
I lifted myself, limped to those woods, woodpeckers with ruby necks,

hectic taps. Stones became my blanket.   ✗
Months later, home, I waited by the side door.
She opened, sighed, a pat on the head and old biscuits enough.   *birth?*

I CAN'T EXPLAIN

Though it is here, in my house, by the keyboard

I plan to give away or the dulcimer with its missing string.

Maybe, the Calla Lilly in the corner of the room,

its needle-shaped crystals of calcium oxalate.

Ask me if it is a blackbird blinking by my window.

Or marshland that began as a pond. I will not tell the truth.

Clarity is definition. *This is who I am, this is my body.*

Five more years of pills, scans. I cover my eyes, see nothing.

THE MATTER OF BEGINNING

I should lug the limbs felled from the storm,
  whole trees at places, pile them beside the road for pickup.
I should empty the cupboard, the kit behind its doors
  that contained a tadpole, never a frog, though ugly.
Before I drag and toss, I should walk a block or two,
  could wave to Laura who slipped a card
  into my mail, *Mercy unto you.*
It is warmer today. I wait to be happy.   *after chemo*
To take off the scarf with the black rose,
  let the sun find the fine hairs beginning.
Someday, today, now, I could slip beside him,
  my misshapen breast tattooed for surgical precision,
  move closer, believe I hear: *Still beautiful.*
Instead, I will read a book about intuitive decisions.
Between reading and crying, wear white in honor
  of yes and no, be a bridge, a bride crossing.

poems of a woman recovering after breast cancer surgery

21

CENTRAL PARK

Behind and in front an ostentation of pink,

she wraps her arm through mine,

irrepressible volunteers, one prepares to cut the ribbon,

cameras ready, I am wrapped in a declaration,

and do you believe, a few women cut in front

as though desperate to sign the forms that state,

unequivocally, yes, we had it,

then across our chests, inscribed on tee shirts,

matching sashes, Survivor, and even that is fine.

This blue-eyed person who once cradled herself

inside my lap, while with the buzz of a lawn moth, I hummed

the first two bars of the song she fell asleep to,

talks to me as though long-lost friends.

Imagine a mother's heavy crystal from Poland,

still not the weight of our possible loss.

And when they cheer, *Look, a Survivor,* I want to shout, "No, lucky,"

but wave beneath an arc of balloons, stagger, dog-tired, to a deli

where other walkers wait in line,

they stopped at the four mile marker,

while we, mother and daughter rule-keepers, needed the full five,

and these others, recognition is almost rescue,

finally my darling and I find a booth for eggs, coffee, strong,

the delight, our sitting down sighs, eating and drinking.

Glass with Soma and Salt

This time there is a window, there is also a sea.

Not what you expect, not my usual ocean of evergreen.

Here I lean against regret.

Behind me, everything I want.

Uncertain blue or insistent green, it is life.

Did you know duck-billed grazers survived the Arctic,

their long May shadows by the Colville River, until they could not?

Here the window is far above, fifteen floors at least.

I stand beside water where salt and wound won't disagree.

Water lifts me, a leaf.

WE TRAVELED TO SEVERAL COUNTRIES

If I lose him, I am afraid I won't hear it again, *Amy.*
I don't remember my mother or father calling, I have lost the sound of them.
Sometimes only footsteps or tapping of two fingers against a white cup calms me.
I know there are people without names, and when he said it, I climbed into it.

In the film, Le Week-End, she almost leaves him, but that is Paris.
This is downstairs, a new TV stand, white plaster board, instructions without words,
drawings and arrows as though a way is always clear.

He knows I know what death before the dying looks like.
I sat with it three times, held its hand.
Each time, its mouth opened while sleeping.

And now when we try to sleep, there is only a small light
in the hall, a child's, and I go toward it
because I don't understand getting older
and because he sleeps far from me.

Anyway, I didn't like France.
At Versailles, the line was long, I was told to return tomorrow,
tomorrow was Chartres.
I asked, "What wine do you recommend? How do I get home?"
Anyway, he longs for Germany, but this is not about travel or hats,
unless it is the hat I wear for the unhurried returning of thin gray hair,
or the trip to another room, in the house we filled.
I was young, wore a velvet beret and a red scarf
I found on a table near Champs-Elysees. I was his red kite.

Toward/Away

Ocean

If I hum, I can't hear you. If quiet, I am you. If I close my eyes, I close the sun. Though I know you are your own thing, with or without me, this is not personal. Here, beside you, he is my missing piece. He waves from the twenty-fourth floor balcony, snaps a photo that looks like a speck, will tell me it is me. I am emptied of everything except love, I had forgotten.

Legs, Walking

You lead me past roses, a purple bush, events that will become history. Girls in huts, schools in flames, then a replicating virus, then water as weapon. When the doctor said the brain cancer had spread I asked, *what cancer,* and understood my mother's sudden sweetness. Disease dug up what she had buried, it did not bring redemption. In the meantime, he sleeps away the morning. When he stands, his legs buckle, unbalanced. He used to walk with me to the river or the market for goat cheese. Legs, you move me toward someone I don't know.

A Year Out

There is a turtle in my mouth.
He is black, beige, stained with surprise.
A slow walker, of course.
Carting himself against the plains
where words erode
in this part of my world, long days of darkness.

He will not be banished.
He doesn't care about the river.
This is his country.
What else do I know?
He moves resolutely from woman to woman,
he will live forever.

2
THE HEALING

WHERE WE LIVE

Home is not where I live,

it is sleeve of a daughter,

hands and green shingles.

Where I do live,

what I can give to you,

to myself, not home exactly,

what remains, beneath the casing.

Each layer whiter than the last.

And the door opens

into a room with a fireplace,

you wait.

This is home. If it is not,

I stoke the fire, listen to the perfect noise

of flightless birds.

ENTRY

First

When traveling, remember small conveniences.
Bring along a collapsible toothbrush.
Fall in love with a soldier, or to be reasonable,
a tour guide, make him dark, exhausted.
Ask questions, imagine a room
overlooking a port, making do.
Ask why your father
longed to live—but did not—here—
beyond Philadelphia's tool and die.
While you are asking, walk into the room,
white quilt, blue mosaics.
This is your bed, your chair.

Friday

Clock tower, taxis, always hummus with oil.
Every building a kind of stone, in and out,
a kind of bleached light.
Call to prayer. Friday dinner, a daughter/soldier
returns. Dogs bark. Exotic howls.
Why do the boys fear the one named Lucy?
I do not cover my head. I cover my body.
Eat figs. Drink black coffee
from thimbles. Cannot get close to the Wall
where I had left a note in '86. Another day,
my daughter says she will slide another note
into its cracks, I have little left to ask for.
Here: soldiers, olives, salt, place.
Soldiers hail a taxi for a man who can't walk,
a meter turned on for a long ride home.

Namal

At the edge of the sea, the port,
where she points out the place
she first ate Shakshuka,
danced in a bar with an indoor pool.
Seagulls dive as they always do, always will.
I am here. On a nearby bench,
breakable as its wooden slats.

Jaffa

Arab neighbors mourn the loss of a mother.
In a yard, on collapsible chairs,
they wave as I pass after a dinner
of forty shared salads with friends.
A man tells me his family has been here for five-hundred years.
I don't know what to say,
we are not maps, nothing leads us to each other.
I shake each hand, talk about weather.
Accept the fig the housekeeper places in front of me,
black coffee, the future.

31

THE STORY OF FIRE

"These are the remembrances of the wakes and the parties,
of the girl pure and fiery who keeps burning underground."
Gabriela Mistral, from *The Shaggy Woman*

She doesn't agree with him, the chef
who assures his listeners: *Fire is masculine.*
Her house is burning.
There is nothing left for her to open or shut, except herself.
She hears everything inside flames.
Everything, memorized.
For the couch, it is the shaved head,
hours of a body hanging on as though a raft.
The couch sighs while remembering because it is sad.
The chair was once surrounded by elegance, not hers,
its green velvet cared for as though a pet.
The table remembers it differently.
It is solid oak, wears scars well.
The rug is jute, sheds into her room,
then into another, where rings of sapphire and amber
are manic stars, and nothing else remains.
The French vitrine, what it holds inside,
what it says to the gold trimmed teacup:
I am here, do not be afraid.
Well, she is afraid. Seductive fire,
articulate rain, all of this being alive.

STONE

Of course it ended up on the sill,

the one that faces the graying

fence. I would like to say I found it

during a meditative stroll, or by a lane,

at a river's roundabout.

But I have given up too much to lie.

I remember I held it in my hand, that is all.

He loved shells and stones.

I can't toss it away with sundry junk.

It might have meaning, I don't know.

BEING SOMETHING ELSE

A window sheeted in plastic and tape,
draped in nothingness like lace.
A window that dreads winter, snow closing us in.
Ice is a reminder.
If there is ever a time to tell the truth, it is now.
I want to go to him, wake him like yeast proofed
to be sure it is alive, winter bread.
He is asleep again.
I kiss his forehead, slip out to make a train.
Before loss, I am loss. I have told no one.
Now I am a train, doors unlocked, passengers
carry fruit.

BEING SOMETHING ELSE #2

Fruit carried to our daughter.
Bananas, green.
When brown with pointlessness,
they are rich with *tumor necrosis factors.*
We move along the same track.
Morning glory thickets beside the train,
their mouths opened, it is early.
I want to sing.
Yes, We Have No Bananas?
No, not that, you sang her to sleep.
A song about us, your legs
awake and wrapped over mine.
I won't leave you, I promise.

SELF AS A BOG

Mostly because in the north, Sundews thrive.
Mostly because lamps cannot evolve
unless taken apart, parts reused.
Hands dictate their function.   (Hands are important.)

The lamp I was given with its ridiculously long neck
by a sister who does not speak to me
hangs above a fifty-year old cracked linoleum floor
covered with wool carpet.

Everything decomposes slowly.
Lack of nutrients force adaptation. A mosquito bites
a left ankle, scans honey beads hanging
deliciously at the Sundew's tip and that is enough.
The Sundew closes, digests. What it lacks
from sphagnum moss, it gains from meat.

(Under the lamp's light, I carefully stitch Moroccan styled
pillows to celebrate a daughter's sixteenth birthday.)

Everyone's life should begin with a stream,
stepping stones, Lucia wearing a green hat,
here is where to begin.
After hundreds of years, in a matter of days,

a bog can be destroyed.
Still, I am rainwater.
I love what is unexpected.
What falls from the sky falls into me.

Still, no one chooses to swim here.
No one longs to curl a hand around
acidic water unmoved for years.
Pitcher plants, Sundews, Great Grey Owls—
They live in spite.

Self as Stand of Maples

Mostly, skinny trunks.

Mostly, I am upright and work too hard at decency.

My leaves are simple, though bear a resemblance to autumn.

If you happen by, while walking with a friend who notices everything,

and you are lathered from head to toe with bug lotion, lugging a water bottle and cell phone,

while the friend you walk with walks ahead, far from the trail to find what you fear,

look into a romance of reds, yellows, you choose.

In the meantime, the friend will discover tiny fish in a muddy body of still water

unable to determine if it is run off or a stream,

though the fish are real, in the meantime, sit with me.

Mostly, be safe.

SELF AS VASE

I am willing to accept galloping cherubs.

Cherubs don't gallop.

They do when afraid of being passé.

The first time I felt reverberations from Forsythia in water.

Now Silver Dollars need nothing.

Is worth guaranteed?

Is that important?

Sell the second Limoges,

Aunt Annie cracked it slightly.

When I listen to Simone's *Sea Lion Woman,*

I become standard azure.

Kandinsky painted *Small Dream in Red,*

hearing sound and color.

I accept my trim of confusion.

TRAIN, BIRD

I only hear birds when the window is opened.
Their songs don't seep through cracks of wood and metal
as they did in the old place.
I don't miss weeping aluminum, stains
on parallel walls.
I miss stumbling into a roomy kitchen,
hearing the complaint of three notes, more necessary than coffee.
I still don't know the name of that bird.
It spoke and answered itself.
Talking to itself, that I understand.

Here, the birds are harder to hear.
The cat is not sure of the train.
It doesn't stop, commotions by.
No trains stop here. Here it comes.

I love it. It is my new wind.
It is a bird talking to my window.
So you need another biopsy. I will
not tell anyone. I will not imagine.
I will learn the art of waiting.
It is hard to love you in three rooms.
Upstairs in the old house I loved the scuffle
of safe shoes.

Here, your fingers flap, birds
against the paper and I want to scream.
Last night we held hands walking the avenue.
It could have been anywhere we have visited
and longed to live.

narrative

*Recurrence of
cancer she doesn't
tell husband
about — he did too?*

39

Fall, Then Winter

Beside me, not the guy that read Princess of Mars to her, what remains.

Cheekbones shifted, he was my Black Irish.

When snow falls, he will insist, his shovel rusted.

Until I am safe, until the signal is sent, smoke or wave, confusion and faith,

damn you, don't leave.

Maples emptying.

An oak with one limb stretching over our lawn, another rising.

BELOW BOILING POINT

I will not tell you
I am writing about nothing.
What is it?
My answer is not to answer.
Even breath is something.
Is it when you walk out of the room?
You are still something, I swear.
Nearly deaf, you cannot hear what I hear,
the almost silent bubbling
along the pan's bottom,
but it is more, something, it is air.

I have been looking out this window for twenty-five years.
Cracked oaks, repeating evergreens,
last winter, a limb thunked on our roof, we needed
someone to climb and remove the giant.
The roof was safe, no damage, we knew damage had been done.
We could not lug the ladder or scale to the second floor.
Our bodies split, between us, the wind blows.

PEACOCK, HOME

No melting snow bucketing beneath old stucco,

only sky until we grow tired of its stars.

We sip Turkish coffee served with sweets,

then walk to the side of town with a gray-green river we have learned to love.

I will say dream again, I always do.

Always, a building that spans a city square.

Desperate to get there, I begin in a basement,

but before the stairs, a pool and inside the pool,

a peacock, iridescent blue and green.

In spite of its beauty, I am afraid it will become cruel.

This has happened before, to beauty.

HARD WORDS WITH LEAVES

A tree, its leaves teach the weather.
"It is shaking," or "It is still."
Open a window, five floors up,
smell the world: dumpsters, trains, his tree.

~

Along the tracks, elsewhere,
bare trees spray-painted fuchsia.
A wall, smothered in pink.

~

Someone had a grand day.
Be glad for her, be glad she found
a color she loves, spoke to the dying.

~

He was called to the office for smacking
his school desk, the boy with red hair,
neither of us knew to be still.
I never told him.

~

It is hard to love with eyes half-closed,
head down, hoping to go unnoticed.
Even now, *I love you,*
are fronds inside my mouth.

THIS IS WHAT YOU DIDN'T SAY
for N.B.

You want to understand the unshaven face,
pajamas worn for a month, head in hands,
not because you want to, because you are drowning
as you yank him toward land.

He held you in the ocean, years ago,
his own head underwater, lifting you above because you could not swim.

This is his, not yours, not your
deep-sea submission, not knowing how to live,
more dangerous than salt in wounds.

Meanwhile, *Get the fuck up*,
you do not say what you feel.
Love the world as I do, you are not him.

How to make someone we love want to live?
This is not a hypothetical question.

Look up depression, look up Freud or Rumi.
It is easier to love the pale stone under your shoe.

… easier to say "My tooth is aching" than to say "My heart is broken."

He is your slipshell of breaking heart.

You are nothing now, or rather, an observer he may not remember.

44

LAMPS

This is a chair.
This is a metal lamp.
I turn the lamp on, take inventory.
When I was a little girl, night after night,
I imagined a funeral, a torn black ribbon
pinned to my blouse.
When I was a little girl, I swore
I would grow wings and fly
over a cruel neighbor's house.
Years later, I imagined a cabin, a black river,
a canoe, a man I almost loved who could not swim.
It is true, I can be anything, anyone.
Now, my husband rests on a chair.
It can be this chair. A chair is a fine item.
It is solid, planted firmly.
It does not have black wings.

~

For now, the lamp is turned off.
We walk the stairs into our room.
A white blanket ripped through by the dog
at the edges, waits.
We are not cold.
Still there is something
right about blanketing ourselves in white.
The walls of our house are sea.
You know the color of a lie.
Of course you do.
What I love most about trust
is how it softens, whitens, slowly.

45

3
WALKING TOWARD CRANES

WALKING TOWARD CRANES

The crane reaches to a red wood railing.
What is he doing? Nothing below him
but Ten Thousand Villages, wooden benches,
the sun a slap, everything else quiet.
Inside I know there are sequins sewn on fabric,
on paper lamps, fish swim toward an ocean.
The crane turns out to be useless.
The operator inches his way down,
the window ledge will have to wait.

Later, I notice it's gone, the balcony gone,
four iron S's left with nothing to secure, nothing to protect.
Long-necked iron lamps
bend to the door I enter: this is the world.
Blue green glass from the West Bank, mindful pillows
with strips of satin leading to its ocean of a button,
an anchor for stitched branches, songbirds from India.
I want to travel, probably won't.
I want to walk into a village where a woman weaves yarn,
squat beside her, not condescending,
not sentimental, but because I am lost.

NOSTALGIA

It is fair to crave a lopsided cardboard box.
Red magic marker daring anyone to enter.
Squatting with Freda on the edge of a quarry,
terrified, your body secretly a lake
trying to rise inside the deep pit.
Necessary to long for both quarry and fear.

Though you were never there, not really,
apart and part, waiting as black ice waits.

The narrow road of your childhood will not collapse,
will not overflow with clear water either.
It is hard to say if everyone is you, on the edge
of a town where you once lived, looking up
at the window with an opened shade
at a sister you have not seen for twenty years,
will not see again, brushing her hair.

WHEN SHE ASKED TO READ MY PALM

I decided, yes I would,
   I didn't know why

I would let her pretend

to tell my future,
   anyone's at that

I didn't know or want to know.

She asked who was sitting beside me.
   No one.

She asked what you need.
   Nothing.

Nothing is what we hold close
   when we are indifferent wind

or, to tell the truth, wind & fear.

I listened to her voice
   a breeze

heard or not, depending on light & temperament

tell me what I didn't need to be told.
   It is you, Elsa.

You, my broken ceiling,
   I listen for my life.

& already knew this, I promise.
   I love your daughter, my niece.

I have always known.

for Gabbi

FAMILY HISTORY/REBA

I cannot be your memory,
scarcely recall the details of today's train ride,
leafless trees spray painted fuchsia, the reach
into a wallet to prove age, as though identity
is the same as being alive.
I want to tell a story, yours. Where to begin?
A ship, bread, money exchanged?
A gas lamp lights a room.
I cannot tell my readers the colors of the room
or what you are thinking.
Don't we move through this world
as though it ends when we are gone?
As it turns out, this isn't a story.
It is a lamentation, what is concealed.
I don't even know myself.

AMERICAN DREAM/LEGACY

Outside the window, a red maple.

Safety moves out in the middle of the night.

You worry, a parcel left behind.

Years ago, all that mattered was moving from Olney to Elkins Park Lane.

The Lloyd Wright rooftop pointed toward stars.

Even the needling to *eat eat* every Friday night.

Pass the potatoes meant *silence.*

You cannot talk about anger.

More than once, room darkening shades before dark.

Once— two pillows, one knee, a circus act, you were seven, applause.

Manacha was a butcher.

She was tall, splendid blue eyes.

She was left behind.

We don't deserve to be alive.

You do deserve.

A window still separates you from the world, sometimes.

Building Collapse

I have decided she is named Ruth and sang alto
second to last in the first row

heavy caved in but not earth exactly
a body mistaken for clothes on hangers
belongs to someone

will she be claimed
flowers have names like Lily of Valley
some you had better not eat
a cavity in the ground may or may not produce blossoms

pretending will definitely not produce flowers
because living as though someone you love has already died
means missing details
the permission to see

what remains of a roof
flues discovered while surveying a chimney
ghosts of weathering
not those ghosts but signs

of missing trim and fragments
of architecture carried off by rats
and then someone says out of the blue

My hand hurts this thumb and there it is
an exact location in the body
the specific location inside
the brain that recognizes the body

noticing lips yes a mouth
our dazzling separateness
how the stranger held her split off leg
isn't it amazing

54

Blessing

This is my story.
These are my characters.
A child calls herself Tree.
A mother named Sue.
They live on the Bayou,
a place I know little about.

In this chapter, they lean
against the trunk of the other,
two Evangeline Oaks, together, separate.

Knowing nothing is beginning over.
The maple between two houses on Barringer
was sparse, hardly noticed, except in the fall
when we lingered on plastic chairs
below a green awning, burst into chicken songs,
Buck Bucking, into dusk.

It wasn't the Bayou.
Flush sidewalks, a fearful park
where the man drove by the bus stop,
his dick in his hand. Margie and I laughed,
it was all we knew to do.
I named him Bill.
A simple name for baffling longing.

On the other side of the park, houses shifted
from attached twins to detached questions.
Marge and I sleuthing behind the bushes
to solve a mystery we invented.

What I have learned today is how a sculptor carved wildlife
and musical instruments from a 30-foot dead oak
on Bayou Street in time for the Bayou Boogaloo.

All I know about repurposing is from leaving my home
of twenty-five years.
Inside the monster dumpster, my mother's silk chair
destroyed by the cat, but not the stained shelves that have become
something else, somewhere else.

When Evangeline was an old woman,
she gave up her search, became a Sister of Mercy,
found her lost love in Philadelphia,
Gabriel, he died in her arms.
Thank you, Mr. Longfellow.

Thank you, amazing world.
In my story, Tree grows up, uses her given name, Lisette.
She might leave, cross brackish water.
What happens next, I don't know.

I know there is another tree that sways
outside my new home, new window.
It tells me when the world is hard,
when it is forgiving.

NOTES

Inside The World

Taiga: A boreal forest or snow forest.

Learning to Float

Taxotere: A chemotherapy drug.

For R

after Muriel Rukeyser: "When I am dead, even then, /I will still love you, I will wait/in these poems/When I am dead, even then/I am still listening to you."
—From Muriel Rukeyser, "Then"

The Sparrow: A science fiction novel, author Mary Doria Russell. (Ballantine Books/Random House, 1996)

This is What You Didn't Say

… easier to say "My tooth is aching" than to say "My heart is broken."
—From C.S. Lewis, "The Problem of Pain" (Harper One, 1940)

Walking Toward Cranes

Ten Thousand Villages: A nonprofit fair trade company supporting disadvantaged artisans in 38 different countries.

ABOUT THE AUTHOR

Amy Small-McKinney is the author of *Life is Perfect* (BookArts Press, 2014) and two chapbooks of poetry, *Body of Surrender* (2004) and *Clear Moon, Frost* (2009), both with Finishing Line Press. Small-McKinney was twice nominated for a Pushcart Prize. She was the 2011 Montgomery County Poet Laureate, judged by poet, Chris Bursk. Her poems have appeared in numerous journals, for example, *The American Poetry Review, The Cortland Review,* and *Tiferet Journal.* Small-McKinney's poems  also appear in two anthologies: *Veils, Halos, and Shackles: International Poetry on the Abuse and Oppression of Women,* Edited by Charles Fishman and Smita Sahay, and *BARED: Contemporary Poetry and Art on Bras and Breasts,* Edited by Laura Madeline Wiseman (Les Femmes Folles Books). Small-McKinney has a Masters in Clinical Neuropsychology from Drexel University, but recently returned to school for an MFA in Poetry and Translation at Drew University's low residency program. She facilitates poetry workshops in Philadelphia.

Glass Lyre Press

exceptional works to replenish the spirit

Glass Lyre Press is an independent literary publisher interested in technically accomplished, stylistically distinct, and original work. Glass Lyre seeks diverse writers that possess a dynamic aesthetic and an ability to emotionally and intellectually engage a wide audience of readers.

Glass Lyre's vision is to connect the world through language and art. We hope to expand the scope of poetry and short fiction for the general reader through exceptionally well-written books, which evoke emotion, provide insight, and resonate with the human spirit.

Poetry Collections
Poetry Chapbooks
Select Short & Flash Fiction
Anthologies

www.GlassLyrePress.com

CPSIA information can be obtained
at www.ICGtesting.com
Printed in the USA
LVOW11s2003270117
522452LV00001B/9/P